To Jeffrey Moussaieff Masson, whose book
The Emperor's Embrace: Reflections on Animal Families and Fatherhood
gave me the concept and material for this book,
and to the Clarke and Williams families, for loving me like their own—G.C.

For my daughter, Paris—B.O.

By Ginjer L. Clarke • Illustrated by Betina Ogden
A Random House PICTUREBACK® Shape Book
Random House 🏠 New York

Text copyright © 2002 by Ginjer L. Clarke. Illustrations copyright © 2002 by Betina Ogden. All rights reserved under International and Pan-American Copyright Conventions. Published in the United States by Random House, Inc., New York, and simultaneously in Canada by Random House of Canada Limited, Toronto.
www.randomhouse.com/kids
Library of Congress Cataloging-in-Publication Data
Clarke, Ginjer L.
Wild dads! / by Ginjer L. Clarke ; illustrated by Betina Ogden.   p.   cm. — (Pictureback)   ISBN 0-375-81449-3
1. Parental behavior in animals—Juvenile literature. [1. Parental behavior in animals.] I. Ogden, Betina, ill. II. Title. III. Random House pictureback.   QL762.C47 2002   591.56'3—dc21   2001019924

Printed in the United States of America   First Edition   April 2002   10 9 8 7 6 5 4 3 2 1
PICTUREBACK, RANDOM HOUSE, and the Random House colophon are registered trademarks of Random House, Inc.

Wild dads take care of their babies in some amazing ways!

One animal dad actually gives birth to his babies—the sea horse! This dad carries the eggs in a pouch on his stomach.

After the tiny sea horses are born, their father keeps them in an ocean playpen of seaweed and rocks.

This colorful fish is a cichlid *(SICK-lid)*. The eartheater cichlid dad does not have a pouch, so he carries the eggs in a different place—inside his mouth! He holds the eggs gently until they hatch.

Afterward, the baby fish can swim off on their own. But at night, they swim back into their father's mouth. He protects them from being eaten by frogs or bigger fish.

The father emperor penguin has only one large egg to care for. He holds it carefully on his feet—not in his mouth. He keeps his egg from touching the freezing cold antarctic ice for two long months while the mother penguin looks for food far away.

The mother penguin returns when the egg is ready to hatch. She holds the fuzzy baby on her feet while the hungry father searches for food. After about one month, the father comes back. The father and mother then take turns keeping the baby penguin warm and cozy.

These sun grebe *(GREEB)* finfoot chicks are cozy, too. They are tucked safely in bags under their father's wings. The sun grebe is the only bird that can carry its babies in the air.

This dad takes his babies flying while he looks for a nice fat fish for their breakfast.

At the edge of a river, a beaver dad helps to build a dam and a lodge for his family. After it is done, he lets his babies hitch a ride on his back while he swims.

When one of the baby beavers falls off, the dad hurries to keep it from drowning. Beaver dad to the rescue!

The prairie dog is a protective father, too. He sits up tall outside his family's grassland burrow to watch for danger.

Later, he takes a break to clean and play with his pups.

After a long day, he kisses his babies good night and they fall asleep together in a pile in their underground den. Sweet dreams, little prairie dogs.

The fox father is a fast, smart hunter. His kits look like puppies when they are born. He will take his kits with him on hunts when they are bigger.

But for now, he goes out at night into the forest and brings back a mouse for the babies to eat.
Yip! Yip! the hungry babies cry out.

The father Arctic wolf brings food to his family, too. He catches and eats a rabbit. Then he coughs the meal up into many piles so the baby wolves have something to eat.

Wolf pups love to play with their father. He paws and nuzzles them to show how much he loves them.

This little orange monkey is a golden lion tamarin. He carries his babies on his back. This can be hard work because golden lion tamarins usually have twins!

Together, they swing through the tall forest trees, playing and looking for fruit.

When the African forest is quiet, the father gorilla cleans his babies. He picks through their fur and eats the bugs he finds. The baby gorillas like to be groomed—it makes them feel safe and calm.

But now it is time for their afternoon nap. No other animals will come near them while their wild dad is around!

The next time you see an animal at the zoo or in the wild, remember that it has a special dad—just like you!